Jouce Barno.

Spirit Life

Spirit Life

Marsha J. Perlman

Enjoy our Nature.
Marsha J Perlman
2009

iUniverse, Inc.

New York   Bloomington

SPIRIT LIFE

iUniverse books may be ordered through booksellers or by contacting:

iUniverse
1663 Liberty Drive
Bloomington, IN 47403
www.iuniverse.com
1-800-Authors (1-800-288-4677)

ISBN: 978-1-4401-0267-7 (pbk)
ISBN: 978-1-4401-0268-4 (ebk)

Printed in the United States of America

iUniverse rev. date: 1/26/2009

For

all life
in our natural world.

"The idea of wilderness needs no defense,
it only needs defenders."

—*Edward Abbey, environmentalist*

Contents

Prologue

Volumes of literature exist to describe the effect of humans on nature. This book expresses the effect of nature on humans. My purpose is to paint the beauty and spirit of one slice of the world I inhabit. The poems, written in southwest Florida, mirror my physical, emotional and spiritual encounters—the surprises, humor and magic I share with creatures of my world—
the sense of joy, peace, renewal and inspiration I receive.

It is easy to bypass nature in our speed to compete and produce. Positive connections with our natural world raise awareness of values far beyond usefulness and service, and become an integral part of our lives...decelerating our planet's destruction.

My two-fold intent, through my poetry, is to encourage an accepting, loving relationship with the Earth and to expand human consciousness. We need fewer people manipulating the earth; more people living in harmony and intimacy with our steadily vanishing environment.

We protect what we know and love. Let us become defenders, and ultimately stewards of our natural resources for our own good, and for future generations.

Part One

"We need the tonic of wildness and nature."

—*Henry David Thoreau, naturalist*

Brief Encounters

In watery-pink light I pedal
south to the shore.

My ears respond to rhythms of the sea—
repetitive gurgling, gulping surf,
threatening and soothing,
shells crunch under footsteps.
Labored starting,
abrupt stalling of fishing boats.
Around me, monochrome gray—

I am captive in this mysterious prison
enveloped in clouds of fog, dense as a muddy lake.
I breathe fragrance of decaying sea life,
taste saturated salt air,
fidget with damp clothes limp as seaweed.
My toes squirm in the cold, incoming tide.

Like a hatching egg, I thrust to free myself,
to see beyond the immediate.
Where are familiar markers—
palm trees, wood docks, sand bars?
I am distraught, ill at ease, impatient.
Why this shortage of endurance, this discomfort?
Why lack of skills to loiter, dawdle, procrastinate?

Sluggish minutes tick.
Gray curtain of mist
mutates to muslin, evaporates.

Sea world appears as images in developing liquid,
magenta, scarlet, fuchsia glow euphorically,
a veiled canvas ready to debut.
Outline of boat raising sails.
Focused sanderlings scurrying behind receding waves.
Alert willet probing tide pools.
Slimy catfish trapped in ripples of wet sand.
Profiled terns facing into gusty wind.
Anhingas showcasing their capes' geometric white mazes.
Impish, spotted ibis diverts my attention
with a game of hide and seek around young mangroves.

I sponge up this pristine morning
splashed by nature's gifts,
hearing the ocean call my name.

Tangled Roots

I am off to settle a wager with myself.
Last time I passed this way
I saw walking trees on the shore,
or was it bright sun engaged in foolery?

I approach the island,
slender mahogany-colored limbs
appear like arched bows walking,
clam-shaped feet edged with oyster shell toenails.
Branches intermingle until herds of visible
impenetrable tangled roots stand firm
in cold, black muck. Red mangrove trees
fringe tropical shore.

I punt alongside to steal an intimate glimpse—
two foraging raccoons, blue heron prints,
below me a school of young fish,
scampering crabs, creeping snails,
tiny shrimp, all sheltered
within tangled roots.
Trunks support horizontal arthritic arms
with gnarled joints like giant knobs of ginger
open, ready to protect against hurricanes.

My thoughts leap to contemporary human roots
interlaced like baskets of unraveled balls of yarn.
Add, subtract, blend, knit.
Create intricate genealogy.
Arms open to nurture life with time
and patience, filter vulnerable amid distractions,
furnish nesting and shelter from intrusions.

My mind and eyes play tricks,
attempt to untangle all the roots,
as Herculean as striving to build
a seaworthy vessel without a blueprint.

If I knew magic:
        I would straighten the roots.

        Chaos.

        Confusion.

        Reverse course.

        Balance.

Blended Feathers

Two alert great egrets
stand with diligence at edge
of low sea wall.
Their feathers blend
with white landscape rocks,
razor-edge yellow beaks
silhouette against orange morning sun,
mysterious golden eyes observe me
leisurely paddling my kayak.

As the sun creeps west
I drift home with incoming tide
steering towards the same concrete wall.
where the two alert great egrets
stand poised and vigilant.

Bird one steps nimbly
away from my direction,
grooms its breast, extends its wings.
Bird two remains rooted
to the embankment.
Unusual, unexpected confidence,
quiet composure for a skittery bird.

Closer   still no movement

and closer   that's it.

The Greatest Show At Sea

Board a tour boat.
Captain increases speed,
maneuvers wake.
A passenger screeches,
"Dolphin on the right!"
Jump up, grab your camera,
see a sleek, silver shape
slicing the sea.

Clap, chuckle, shout, stamp.
Twinkling eyes, smiling face,
swirling through waves, surfing the breakers,
vaulting to your height, vanishing below.

Vigilant. This time you shout,
"Dolphins puffing on the left and the right!"
Circling, prodding youngsters at play
encouraging passengers—be child-like too.

Cutting through the water in unison,
springing, diving, rising then disappearing
to the rhythm of a laughing, applauding audience.

Maneuvering

Wake up, they chirp in bird-speak, it is spring.
From their roost on the power lines
lacing the air with songs,
lyrical waves of sound flow
from the mouths of male cardinals,
modeling blazing red suits and caps.
Nearby, one lone singer,
a tireless gray mocking bird
cackling, gurgling, whistling,
screaming, weeping, trilling,
six-movement chorale streaming
from her bellowing lungs.

I slide into my blue boat,
express-paddle to reach the breakfast-needy
outsmarting veteran fishes.
Standing knee-deep in the marsh,
with a hypnotizing stare, focusing on the black water
one great blue heron poised,
primed to bayonet his feast.

Relaxed piloting through mangrove arch
into a round lake.
Young kingfisher slips off tapered branch,
flaps to right itself,
dives headfirst, spears small snapper.

In the distance, plump mullets
appearing like Olympic gymnasts
leap and tumble across the water.
I no longer try to catch them,
shrimp bait doesn't tempt these vegetarians.

High-noon rays sizzle like drops of
cold water meeting a red-hot griddle.
I change course and coast through nature's
cathedral, along the center aisle
of overlapping, over leaning branches,
glimmers of sunlight spilling onto
ruffling water, doors of long roots dangling
above me, snakes ready to dive—
not into my boat, please.

Loud snuffles from a pair of round,
brown-flared nostrils grasp my attention,
lumbering manatee looking up at me,
traveling alongside my boat to rhythm
of downtempo paddle.
Vanishing under my kayak, lifting
me gently out of the water, then
gradually sliding me down her sloping back.

Unspoken mystical message
delivered with love,
forever alters me.

Legal Limit

I inflate the yellow balloon,
tie it to my line,
hook large chunks of ladyfish,
cast lengthy distance from the powerboat.

Balmy weather, tepid water
ideal conditions for catching shark.
Not JAWS, three to four-feet of
first-rate eating, I am told.

I munch pretzels, drink pop, stare, wait,
track speck of color
jiggling and bobbing
among the waves.

The balloon disappears.
Cue—I jump.
Grab the sturdy pole, yank the line,
reeling tough, muscles taut,
scoop into jumbo net, unload into red cooler,
pull up the anchor and head home.

Mr. O!

Please Mr. Osprey, tell me why
you spend your days up so high.

Perched on a rod of my neighbor's antennae,
alone except with a fish for dinna'.

Last three winters I awakened to your tune,
handsome, silhouetted against full moon.

Impressive bird, robust and clean,
you catch the largest trout I've seen.

Do you notice females pass you by,
do you always wonder why?

Is it because you have no nest?
Roost with you? What a jest.

You're unprepared as a mate,
A future husband? You don't rate.

Hurry friend construct proper house,
so you can entice this charming spouse.

Fury

Two kayaks, one blue, one green
hastily transformed into graceful vessels.
Fishing rods, bait, stringer, anchors, lunch, water.
Azure sky, wispy clouds,
soft breeze, mini-ripples.
We head west.
Paddling and fishing, a new adventure.
My first cast, a red, white, and green fish?
No, a bouquet of sea grass.

Change direction, aim south.
Explore mangrove islands.
Manta rays scatter, oystercatchers huddle
on fast vanishing sand bar.
Shrewd pelicans surround,
eyes riveted to fishing lines.

Without a heartbeat of warning
blustering wheels of wind descend.
Swells, white caps, thermometer plunges,
black clouds bulge obliterating sun.

Swerve toward shore,
Paddle faster, paddle stronger.
            "I cannot do this."
Paddle stronger, paddle faster.
            "I do not have the strength."

My partner encourages, reassures.
Water laps against my boat.
Splashes over my bow.
Wind intensifies.
Energy-charged waves increase in height.
Arms, like my breathing, shift to automatic.

"What is this? I'm moving backwards!"
As challenged as Sisyphus, I am struggling
in my uphill climb to shore.
Sweat blinds me. I am terrified.
Persevere.
Paddle.
Pray.
Eyeglasses drip salt.
Blur of colors.
Ghostly shapes loom.
A mirage?
Water depth decreasing?
Loss of senses?
Disoriented.

I cannot move.
I cannot speak.
I cannot breathe.

Shades Of Mango And Melon

I scope the best site.
Stand my tripod in the shallow surf.
Sit on my folding stool.
Snack on a strawberry sandwich.

Young children run from ripples
insisting they are waves.
I laugh.

People arrive by car, golf cart, bike,
kayak, canoe, foot, for one-of-a-kind
color ceremony of blended spices and fruits.

I focus on the western sky.

Paisley designs
in shades of mango and melon
vacillate into apricot and tangerine.

Shafts of squash and pumpkin tones suspend
from swollen cumulous clouds, twist
into new shapes, burst into undulating
ribbons of papaya and peach,
stretching further than I can see.

A glowing orange and persimmon volcano
spits fire from edge of the ball of light,
through deep purple clouds,
glitters burnished gold column
along the water, directed at me.

Sun slumps below horizon.
Ceiling explodes into flames,
mingled paprika, pomegranate and saffron.

Guess

There on the dock
three birds stand,
stare, scope, wait
with frozen patience
for their prey.

A tall, stately great blue heron,
an alert, great egret,
a slender, tricolor heron.

Silently, I guide my kayak toward them.
Which will be first in flight?
The smallest?

I observe, not waiting long.
Great blue extends her neck
elevates her tall, sleek body
crosses the canal.
Egret flaps his expansive wings
follows close behind.

Alone, tricolor persists
in search for an elusive fish.

Jubilant Summer World

Standing alone,
somber, silent, desolate,
under black sky of winter world.
Twisted thoughts
stretching, straining like
germinating seeds, restless growth.
Searching for stream of light
to assure new day is dawning
to transform dreams, to alter life's design.

Mauve streaks slyly emerge,
dividing sky and water,
rose, crimson, gold
exploding fireworks onto fluid palette,
brush clouds into shapes and figures.
Blood-orange erupts,
ball of fire cascading to earth
awakens the universe, spawns warmth.

Harmony of song.
Chorus of laughter.
Duet of love.

Private Performance

My reserved seat: flat brown rock.
Backdrop: sky, clouds.
Stage: sand and gulf,
Props: mangroves, sea grapes.
House Rule: Once Seated, Do Not Move.

Little blue heron with pencil-thin neck
dancing solo ballet for me.
Knee-deep in surf, head leading
deliberate, measured steps.

Exaggerates elevated toes, increasing pace
running across stage left to right,
unfolded wings flapping,
leaps unsupported, spins a three-sixty
alights delicately.
Pauses.
Pivots.
Poses.
Repeats dance identically,
this time right to left.

Sun descends, tide reaches high,
she circles me, ascends to fly.

Stingray Shuffle

Gliding the warm, ocean floor,
I'm a sassy, swimming saucer.
When humans approach
and continue to encroach,
I become a double-crosser.

A venomous barb on my tail,
poses potential danger.
My personal protection
guarantees your dissection,
you seacoast amateur.

Here's my advice to you,
for eluding my under-sand ruffle.
Wade near the shores
to eliminate stressors,
      and—

Dance the Stingray Shuffle.

Part Two

"One should lie empty, open, choiceless as a beach—
waiting for a gift from the sea."

—Anne Morrow Lindbergh, author
Gift from the Sea

Speechless

Rustling leaves.
Rasping branches.
Pine limbs separate.
Muffled thump.

I spring from my bike—
        Startled.
An adult bald eagle—
        Stands.
Three-feet from me.
Diligent yellow eyes.
Powerful outstretched wings.
Ominous anchored talons.

Stunned into silence
I gape at her
she gawks at me—
seconds feel like minutes.

She engages her wings.
Raises her plump body.
Sidles between branches.
Glides on thermals.
Oversees her kingdom.

Mesmerized.
I blink
and pedal away.

Bird School Is Tough

Making morning rounds
stopping at each family's home
is part of my daily routine.

Today I hear abrupt screaking and squawking,
loud, quick-tempered bird-talk.
Mother osprey on nearby roof
oversees her three chicks and shouts
impatient, emphatic orders.

Oldest offspring stands at edge of
nest staring downward, mobilizing courage
knowing what is expected of her.
Flapping wings, taxiing, lifting off,
skimming treetops and chimneys.
Gleeful singing, eventually deplaning
on sharp pinnacle of tall,
bronze weathervane.

Sudden, merciless wind
gyrates the bird at dizzying
speed. Talons clenched, she
teeters to maintain balance.
Glee transforms to shrill.
Shrieking pierces the air.

Minutes hang heavy,
wind abates,
chick flies short-cut home
hunkers down between siblings.

Bargain Hunters

Fresh fish sighted.
Yellow and white heads orbit,
plummet, webbed feet brake.
Fourteen pelicans gather in turbulent water
clamoring and swooshing, twenty-eight eyes
staring at angler filleting day's catch.
Daring bird hops onto piling, dock, boat.
Another follows aggressively edging closer.
Birds open formidable bills, seize tossed scraps.

Fierce competitive feeding.
Extended long necks, jostle rivals,
clacking, unyielding beaks, never sharing,
never caring, never satiated.
Victors chomp, losers squawk,
persistent until last piece is devoured.

On cue, bodies lift, follow sixth sense
to repeat boisterous quest.

Super clothing sale advertised.
Compete for parking space, sprint into line,
doors open, scurry inside,
elbow rivals, shove into position
of advantage: snatch, scrutinize, secure.

Fierce competitive shopping.
Clerks refresh dwindling stock,
contrast styles, sizes, prices,
persistent until final item is purchased.
Homeward bound, display, admire
possessions, regret overlooked possibilities,
next week's flyer delivered.

On cue, unsaturated minds and bodies lift
to repeat boisterous quest.

Surrender

Today, discouraged gray sky replaces
  yellow light of morning, opening its arms and
  tossing out its burdens, howling thunder,
  black tears falling in sheets
  beating the coarse pavement like the
  crescendo of an orchestra's tympani section.

A distorted form with bamboo-like legs
  plods in my direction through fog, then stops.
  Harley, our great blue heron.
  I barely recognize you without feathers
  neatly combed, erect stance, graceful "S" curve.

You greet me with a mottled body,
  clumps of shaggy, matted plumes,
  hunched shoulders. Crouched on squat wood fence,
  as if you took an unwilling dive
  into the sea, or left your nest this day
  without wearing public clothes.

Here I sit, warm and dry
  gazing through streaked window panes,
  drops of water converting to puddles
  joining to form rivulets. Need I remind you
  I never feed wild birds?

The air drips gray.
       You advance, then anchor yourself on the
       outside table staring at me with steely eyes.

You nurture me with hours of entertainment
crisscrossing the sky with hoarse croaks,
pilfering from shrimp buckets,
absconding with freshly caught fish.

I cannot turn away from you.

Tenacious Catfish

Fish line nosedives, arm jerks up.
Hooked a big one, I start reeling.
Powerful fish tugs, drags the filament.
One side   other   under   behind.
Fail to shake it, knife out of reach.
I squirm, struggle to follow.
Kayak surges, anchor lodged.
Dragged across lake.
Rod in holder strains at right angle.
Attempt to paddle, abandon challenge.
Sturdy boat veers into blustery wind.
Fish acquires strength, I grow weary.
Jettison rod? Leap from boat?
Fishing partner speeds.
Intercepts my vessel, severs line.

Sighs of relief dissolve into laughter.

Water's Edge

My favorite time of day is morning,
not just any morning,
a warm, foggy morning at low, low tide,
pre-dawn before first sliver of light.

I set my sandals on a mound of rocks.
Squishy-sounding steps on carpet
of cold, hard then soft sand,
to reach ankle-deep wrinkled sea.
Alone, distant sounds of rolling surf
fuse ghostly and supernatural solitude.

Scanning the sky, layers of pinks and
purples begin unfolding into
yards of flowing silk,
reds and yellows oozing behind clouds
igniting wet sand into sea of tropical art.

As fog dissipates, birds come into view,
greeting me with clamorous chatter.
Pelicans and plovers posing on gravel spit.
Little blue heron and snowy egret fishing,
stepping cautiously among their reflecting images,
skittery birds frame arc around me,
weary birds assemble on pilings,
transfixed new arrivals scrutinize me.

"Gamble, I am low-risk."

My cold feet lead toward warm shoreline,
pausing at schools of luminous minnows,
limpid, amorphous jellyfish, raccoon prints,
tidal pools created in deep human footprints,
cozy conchs anticipating incoming tide.
I stroll, shoulders rounded,
big toes over-turning shells, uncovering
partially submerged palm fronds, stones, roots.
I stoop, retrieve a treasure, today a lone pink feather,
other times a vacated sand dollar, sea star,
or horseshoe crab shell.

Riprap seizes my attention,
stacked with weathered cavities,
each miniscule apartment houses
one, tiny snail clinging adamantly,
waiting for high tide to return.
Osprey pair swoops close to my shoulder,
snatches beet-red seaweed, bolts toward nest.
Fitful movement along compacted sand unveils
flawless chiseled holes piercing the beach,
fiddler crabs scurrying to their underground city.

Keen to examine last night's spill,
I contemplate how far coconuts traveled
to line the waterfront,
where seedpods, leaves, and buds began their journey,
how many nights berries and limes were
prodded and pushed on their ride.
What prompted building materials to join this voyage?

Fishing boat rumbles, signals time to leave
gentle shore meeting dramatic sea.
Tonight, when birds walking on my roof awaken me,
I will listen to incoming tide polishing the coast,
nourishing sea life.

Speculating on all I will uncover tomorrow
at low, low tide.

Room And Board

Pairs of eyes
fused to binoculars
swiveling skyward,
tracking high-pitched
screeches to interwoven
twigs and trash residence
precariously positioned
at treetop.

Male osprey's
powerful talons
release thrashing trout.
Female shreds fish,
chews, nourishes
two screaming chicks.

Pulse of life predictable.
Like dog-eared pages
of a timeworn script
rewound and replayed.

Durable family
seldom seen
in today's human world.

Recycled

Sign reads: PLEASE TAKE ME.
"What I need without a fee."

Inflate tires, oil chain,
proceed for test ride on local lanes.

Chrome wheels go round and round,
rusted, dented over uneven ground.

Frozen gears, but brakes work well,
one speed perfect, seat— comfort gel.

I add a mirror for safety, odometer for ego,
basket for notebook, water bottle below.

Red lights blink on roads when dark
at sunrise, sunset, wherever I park.

Through gravel, mud, sand, crushed shells,
trails or pavement, it carries me well.

I travel the Island, thrive on exploring,
up and down byways, no traffic roaring.

Proudly sharing hours of time,
with two- and four-legged friends of mine.

Rabbits, turtles, armadillos to see,
peacocks, foxes, deer roam free.

Longer days, greater delight,
fortunate find…. Island bike.

Cooperative Fishing

They arrived in January by commercial jet
wearing white fur coats
and leggy orange boots,
four, adult white pelicans
rescued from northern ice.

One early March afternoon,
I visit their new home,
forty-birds identically attired,
positioned in horseshoe formation,
synchronized swimmers preparing
for their daily performance.

Thrashing wings, churning water,
silently, steering panicked prey
into shallows.
In hypnotic unison all beaks
point down, all tails point up,
fishnet pouches
snare, scoop, sieve,
necks lift skyward, swallow the bounty.

Here I stand, observing—
a rare, steadfast ritual
immune to our turbulent world.

Nesting

Winter Solstice.
I arrive at this public, obscure location
before dawn.
Position myself in a line of tripods,
topped with cameras securing lenses
longer than my arm, all aiming
at one pair of herons standing in full view,
firing flashes, snapping shutters
two to five times a second.

Birds continue appearing.
Nimble snowy egrets first.
Leggy great blue herons follow.

Males stake claim to roosting site
on green, shrub-covered rookery,
encircled by narrow moat,
trapped by urban life.

So begin my weekly excursions.

I focus on an upright male's
effort to attract a mate.
He meticulously preens each lengthy quill,
executing courtly bow surrounded
by his feathery skirt, then rises,
pumping his elongated neck skyward,
vocalizing a soulful call.
Repeating, repeating—

Abbreviated courtship.
Both present sticks,
clasp each other's bills.

Male flies to mainland,
gathers branches, returns,
transfers to female—beak-to-beak—
she the architect, interior decorator,
weaver of flat, rimmed nest.
Mate scrutinizes, pokes a few twigs,
quickly mounts partner from behind
in crouching position, for three or four seconds,
flaps his wings, airlifts to collect more sprigs.
Mating herons recorded by camera clicks.

Female sits upright, alert. Male flies in,
pecks mate, she fishes, he sits.
There's no time for me to count the eggs.
For three weeks, I wait, anticipate.

Mother is standing,
looking down at two furry balls.
Father arrives with food, female chews,
regurgitates into chicks' mouths.

Subsequent visit, pace increases,
building an addition to their nest,
and continuous feeding of squealing youngsters.
Each week chicks sharpen skills,
flap, nap, snap, thrusting their
bills into parents' beaks.
Two months within the parameter
of their one room dwelling.

Rookery transforms to high-rise dwelling,
New arrivals squeeze into available space,
cacophonous racket ensues.
Mature youngsters croak,
ruffled feathers threaten
intruders intersecting imaginary
territorial line.

Daily when the sun flows over the trees,
birds compress themselves onto their nests,
I stow my gear
and retreat until next week—

unless curiosity overrides my calendar.

Oblivious

Stationary as a sculpture
I stand tall,
my attention directed at a
tricolored heron dining solo
as all herons do.
Wading belly-deep in water
she darts to the right,
with a rapid about-face
hesitating long enough
to thrust her extended, slender neck
into the muddy channel.

Wings outspread
for shade to lure.
Her head upsprings,
silver minnow wiggling in long, honed bill.
Standing tall,
quick swallow, she scurries away.

"Is that a smile I see on your face?"

Gathering

ESSENTIALS:
>Three wire cage traps
>with weighted bottoms,
>braided rope knotted to white foam buoys.
>fish guts or chicken necks seduce,
>one-way traffic ensnares.
>Attach traps to pilings or situate in open water.
>
>Three days later, muscular arms retrieve.
>Tongs arrest aggressive pincers as
>cobalt males are detained in an oversized bucket,
>females returned to the sea.
>
>Twelve blue crabs guarantee
>adrenalized, vivacious feast.

DIRECTIONS:
>Boil water in crab pot.
>Add crustaceans into basket.
>Layer with pulverized seafood seasonings.
>Steam for 30minutes.
>Remove red-ready crabs.
>Chill for several hours.

DELEGATE TASKS AS FRIENDS ARRIVE:
>Cover outdoor table with thick layer of newspapers.
>Create a colorful centerpiece including
>vertical rolls of paper towels,
>orange and red-flowered bowl heaped with coleslaw,
>assorted drinks and a rubber-handled hammer.

At each setting, plate, fork, glass,
nutcracker and pick.

Sit around the table,
pass copious plate of crabs.
Wide eyes examine,
hesitant hands select one.

Heads turn toward the hostess.

She lifts the hammer
and cracks, fractures, splinters
the first crab,
pitching shells into waiting buckets.

Amid hilarity and chatter—
Attack, smack, whack.
Grab, jab and excavate.
Nibble, chomp, gorge.

Savor.

Eight Days A Week

Adopt the lifestyle of an osprey parent?
Are you jesting?
Perched on eggs at the summit of a telephone pole,
fishing all day, racing to satisfy hunger,
screeching as deafening as a locomotive whistle,
as much pleasure as living in a mega-city.

But ospreys are more than a squeal and a shout,
they are devoted parents without a doubt.

Mom patiently roosts for thirty-five days,
Dad dives for fish, keeps enemies at bay.

Flying, fishing, bird school is rough,
focused on brood, overworked and gruff.

In four weeks chicks approach full size,
another eight and each one flies.

As adults they are pressured to GO,
not welcomed back, empty-nesters say NO.

How does this sound to parents stressed,
working 18 years to do their best?

Saturated with complaints, often with groans,
surprisingly, kids may never leave home.

We've become part-time parents is what I read,
supplying love, providing feed.

Less concentration, more dissatisfaction,
disposable commodities, instant gratification.

Poverty, abandonment, violence, crime,
headline the news time after time.

Must do extra psychologists say
what are we missing?
An eighth day.

Adopt the lifestyle of an osprey parent?
An idea as foolish as wearing a clown
costume to a black-tie dinner.

Instead of—
sensible,
logical,
practical,
          what fun to be half-witted.

Part Three

"Think of all life on Earth.
We cannot afford otherwise."

—*Tiite, contemporary artist*

No Wake Zone

Gentle giant in the water.
Docile yet observant,
unobtrusive yet supportive.

Without warning she is thrust
into the spotlight,
attacked, sliced with a propeller
from a speeding watercraft
for reasons unknown to her.

She sees the whirling steel masks,
the single riveted emotion,
the conflicted vicious, noxious rage.

The manatee retreats to her tranquil canal
with baby for comfort.
One step closer to complete withdrawal.
Distraught.
Need for survival.
Intuits.

A time of doubt.

Would I have fared better
by continual tail trouncing,
repetitive body revolutions,
high-velocity swimming?
         she asks herself.

Panthers In The Park

Do I see raised eyebrows in this group?
I expressed nothing obscene, no radical ideas,
All I said is that I love to go camping,
tent camping in the Keys.

On hard ground?
        Your mind can't be sound.
Crawling out, crawling in?
        You'll wear your knees thin.
Aren't you scared of the dark?
        There are panthers in the park.
A day without a shower?
        I wouldn't last an hour.
Can you lock your tent?
        This isn't worth a cent.

I look around campgrounds
At the young people in glee,
Rarely a streak of gray hair
No one who looks like me.

It's always unique and enchanting
To see the first rays of light,
Peeking out the screen door
Magnificent, dazzling sight.

Pink puffs of sugared whipped cream
Float across the sky,
Vivid flowers, lofty pines
With silence issuing a sigh.

Need I act as others
Expect me to at my age?
I'm having too much fun this year,
not ready to turn the page.

Kismet

Wind frenzied and relentless.
Dried seed-pods feverishly rustling
sounding like brass chimes
reverberating in a Zen garden.
Wild air raging
day into night.
Branches like waving arms
of a boater in distress.
Angry forces howl.
Shelter to winged creatures,
shade for two-footed.
She struggles to fulfill her destiny.

Duped

See them, river color, swimming leisurely,
their bulging eyes above surface.
Observe them, sprawled on beds of dry grasses
along steep river banks,
waddling in and out of fresh water,
four-foot, ten-foot, fifteen-foot
alligators whose habitat I am entering by kayak.

Late afternoon, three robust
strokes propel me onto shore
of a windswept lake.
My left foot almost touches the ground,
my peripheral vision glimpses movement.

Racing from the water on all four legs,
his cavernous jaw displaying bone crunching
teeth, high-speed swinging tail,
hissing, grasses mashing between us.

Heart thumping, trembling, vigilant,
I fall backwards into my boat,
and pull in the rope, safety vest, paddle.

Gator pauses within reach of the bow,
swivels, then bolts towards assertive tourists
armed with cameras and surplus sandwiches
clicking, tossing, laughing
at gathering of mature alligators.

Ignoring posted signs warning of provoked aggressions.

Exodus

Barely a foot of grass
stretches between us.
She pecks among the summer blades
over-spilling her beak with snippets
of white dandelion down.
I recline in one chair.
She settles on the arm of another,
eyes riveted on me.
Entrapped by her attention,
the scrub-jay treads delicately
in my direction, lifts her wings and
never looks back.

To The Queen

Jump on your bike
come ride with me
down a long, quiet road
we'll take time to see.

Where gravel meets grass
hibiscus bloom profuse,
strip mall meets mangroves
we need no excuse.

Look—doe standing still as a piling
staring at something intently,
I circle around, she does not budge
no fear apparently.

Meadow stirs with motion and zest.
Tiny head pops up then another—
twin-spotted fawns tumble and topple.
Doe transforms to mother.

A graceful leap across the road,
nuzzling, stroking from the Queen,
knows what she was born to do—
Can you visualize this scene?

We stop—enjoy their interplay
frolicking, nibbling flowered bush,
soon it's time to start for home
Queen Mother nudges gentle push.

We'll continue biking to the end of this road
eyes following nimble deer,
floating towards trees, flowers, grasses.
Regal stance, silent hooves   disappear.

Dinner Theater On The Sea

Dropping my anchor
leaning back in comfort,
I focus on acrobatic
hunters at work.

A lone pelican plunge-dives
scoops baitfish, extracts water
raises pouch and swallows rapidly.

A white ibis pecks tenaciously
in mud, decurved red bill
amasses small critters.

One skittish great blue heron floats out of the clouds,
traverses the lake with a gravelly grunt,
as a human threatens its fishing hole.

Sailing cormorants propel rapidly
under water, hooked beaks
grasp fishes, snakes, eels.

Great egrets twelve-feet apart
pacing, scanning low banks,
spearing hapless, immature mackerel.

Male osprey plummets, plucks trout.
Flips fish forward
speeds toward his nest.

Sitting on the fringe for hours, delighting in
a star-studded performance, contemplating—

Will a famine one day
end this dramatic show?

I Say Nay

One jumping mullet, then another,
maybe father chasing mother.

Over the bow of my boat they go,
Cannot catch them, I am slow.

They have no fear, terrible tease,
I am laughing loud as I please.

Off to the co-op, buy two fish,
back home I cook a tasty dish.

Oil, spices, filets in a pan,
fry them crispy as I can.

Guests compliment delicious treat,
I stare at my plate, unable to eat.

Are these the playful fish from the water?
If so, eating is an impossible order.

What's wrong, friends ask, feeling ill?
No, I sigh, I've had my fill.

Pausing On A Dead Tree Branch

I follow shrill, penetrating shrieks
to the crook of a sturdy tree branch.
At home in their nest,
two adults and one full grown youngster
flutter and chatter.
It's Spring—fledge-time,
when parents hustle to complete lessons.

Three quiet ospreys fly
one behind the other.
The lead bird curves right, all follow,
repeating the drill five times.

Why are they doing this?

Day 2: The female osprey glides
          three-feet above the water,
          chick trailing closely.
          Male brings up the rear.

Day 3: Mother guides, quivers, feet skimming water,
          young osprey dips, misses his mark.
          Father scolds him.

Day 4: Her feet immerse in deep canal,
          their son rises before water contact.
          Dad imparts a discordant reprimand.

Day 5: Juvenile follows mother,
        both dunking their talons into the sea,
        junior retracts quickly, whimpers.
        Parents softly bird-speak.

DAY 6: Inexperienced fellow shadows,
        while his father hovers, dives feet first,
        grabs flounder, escorts family to their habitat.
        Mother rips pieces for breakfast.

Day 7: Each parent plucks, then releases catch.
        Their immature osprey preens close by,
        roosting on nearby branch.

Day 8: Insistent yelping,
        as offspring pleads for breakfast
        and grown-ups face away.
        Novice takes flight between mom and dad,
        plummets, grasps three-inch pinfish.
        Gleeful trills, the household retreats to their refuge.
        Parents supervise beginner devouring his prize.

Day 9: Family soars to bay, perches on tall branches.
        Youthful bird lunges, talons clench snapper,
        pilots kin to their dwelling
        with joyous chirps.

Day 10: Parents and child navigate to nearby
        mangrove key, settle on leafed treetop,
        adults twitter, youngest osprey nosedives,
        seizes bulky sheepshead amid
        continuous, loud screeches.

Day 11: Dad and mom sit in their snug residence,
        the younger, mature bird stands on the rim,
        looks down then out.
        He flies to a tree,
        sparkling, silver ladyfish
        swims slowly, searching for food.
        Bold bird swoops and snatches
        as a trio of high-pitched squeals fill their sanctuary.

Day 12: The adroit angler sits on a dead tree branch
        annihilating a sea trout's head—
        one eye at a time.

Circle Of Life

Muffled high-pitch wail.
Loud and relentless, stabbing
my ears while I walk at daybreak
through dense, shoulder-high palms.

Rest stop under thatched shelter
liberates my curiosity.

I look below me, nothing.

I look above me, something.

Yellow rat snake's body rigidly
coiled around roof's
horizontal support pole,
tail dangling like a vine.
Pocketsize yellow-green toad,
head and forearms twitching
from snake's overstretched mouth
bit by bit, torturously consumed.

Squeals.
           Silence.

Ruby Red

I slow-drive north along narrow, serpentine beach road,
following a birder's hand-drawn map
to locate feeding grounds.
Window open, eyes darting left.
The slurping surf, early summer breezes
and warm sunshine tranquilize me.
Patient motorists crawl, I shift onto grassy lane.

Rounding a corner, a blizzard of vivid rose-hued feathers
generates high-impact splashdown.
Ostentatious arrival of six rare roseate spoonbills.
Stunning waders slosh in shallow
vegetation-choked bay.
Pairs of sparkling, ruby red eyes stare at me
from baldheads.

Brilliant plumes stretch a wing's length apart.
Long, wide, wooden-spoon-shaped bill tips submerge,
heads sweep side to side, probing
for tiny fishes, beetles, crustaceans
detected by sensory intuition.
Beaks snap shut.

Breakfast completed, birds stroll the shore.
As abruptly as they touched down, elegant birds
extend their wings, climb invisible ladder of air.
Patterned pinks shade to crimson, darken to grape,
flying in one column, flapping and gliding in unison.
Exquisitely backlit against cobalt sky.

King Of The Kill

Honor them or loathe them.

Bald, red- and black-faced vultures
foraging for blood, guts and death.
Putrid carrion—their comfort food.

Wind is home to beasts
hundreds of feet high
with flapless wings
cruising currents, circling,
banking, drifting, dipping.
Like translucent paper fans
their wing tips open and close.

Ignited by stench of a meal.

Sanitizing the earth.

Spiraling Inward

Delicate snowy egret, slim alert
circling me as I sit, like a gentle little flirt.

In the waning shade of my young grapefruit tree
pen to paper, writing what life means to me.

Your perimeter grows smaller each time I raise my head,
if it's a fish you're after, here you won't be fed.

Increasing steps exercise golden bamboo feet.
What will I do when your plumage and I meet?

Your sprinting grows faster, it is almost a run.
How much closer to center do you plan to come?

You ignore what I am saying, you're as quiet as can be,
intent on a goal, what it is I'll wait and see.

Those circles are not dance steps you are creating,
if you were a person, I would feel a berating.

I see a labyrinth with me in the center,
you, my friend, appear ready to enter.

Am I exaggerating all I am receiving?
Ignoring would be a monochromatic weaving.

How do I begin on this journey, on this course?
Disregarding opportunity, an unthinkable loss.

No coincidence we are both here today,
astonishing white bird, show me the way.

Your message is brilliant, what introspection must I begin?
Moving outward to inward, from beyond to within.

Reaching for answers, risking inch by inch,
exploring life's mysteries, not nearly a cinch.

I have tasted life's bitters, cherished life's sweets,
trudged rough roads in my bare feet.

Stretched in jubilations, corralled deep despairs,
kindness and compassion, always portions to share.

There remain many questions whose answers I seek,
this pilgrimage not for everyone, not for the meek.

Thank you little egret for sharing my quest,
I am no longer alone in this surmountable test.

I will never completely know what life means.
Our place in the scheme of the Infinite does not resolve,
so it seems.

No Name, No Sign, No Parking Space

Timid steps cross creaking branches,
crackling dried palm fronds.
I shift aside a branch or two
and slip in.
Facing me, an oval, fresh-water
pond surrounded by sky-bound pines.

Feathered wading residents gliding
on airstream spiral downward.
Dressed in formal white, they flaunt their finery—
Wood storks wear black wing stripes.
Snowy egrets model golden slippers.
Ibis display red bills and black wing tips.
Great egrets sport orange beaks.

I am an interloper perched on a crumbling stump
partially hidden, not daring to wiggle,
scratch, or shift position, elated
to witness vitality of bird life,
listen to cacophony of their songs.

Great egrets and chicks
splashing, preening, chittering.
Tree limbs weighted with yelping ibis
drying unhinged wings.

Twittering snowy egrets strutting, then gracefully
hopping onto partially submerged boughs.
Solemn wood storks in stoop-shouldered posture
perhaps contemplating bird-world problems.

Shadows crawl down towering trees,
signaling arrow-formation
coloring the sky white.

Exodus.

Epilogue

Shadows amplify catastrophic paradox.
Steadfast energetic environmentalists
rescued handsome wildlife from extinction—
No ornamental plume hunters.
No DDT softening immature eggshells.
`No Hunting' signs displayed.

Burgeoning species deliver—
       colors to our world,
       songs to our ears,
       smiles to our faces,
       calm to our psyches,
       joy to our lives.

We reciprocate by—
       amputating our forests
       eradicating their food sources,
       razing their natural homes,
       eliminating their ponds,
       demolishing their safe places.

Creatures around me
can not create changes, can not control,
do they want to, would they if they could?

They adapt or expire.

While arrogant humans believe themselves
deserving and capable of manipulating the natural world.

Our work begins…again.

"Never doubt that a small group of thoughtful people
can change the world—
it is the only thing that ever has."

—*Margaret Mead, anthropologist*

Acknowledgments

My thanks to:

—Members of Pine Island Writers and Peace River Critique Circle for their feedback on a selection of these poems.

—Sheilana Massey and Lynne Mayhew for generously reading my manuscript and offering perceptive comments.

—Gene Rossman—enthusiastic and skilled naturalist—for introducing me to Florida and sharing his expertise about the environment, past and present.

—A Room of Her Own—Retreat for Women Writers, Ghost Ranch, New Mexico—for igniting the spark.

—Elizabeth Farrellee, iUniverse, Inc., for her patient assistance throughout the publishing process.

Many, many special thanks to Joyce Daniels and Jeannette Batko for our weekly, tenacious critique sessions at our table by the sea, always sprinkled with humor, food and visiting sea life.

Front Cover Photograph: *Great Egrets Build Their Nest* by author, copyright 2008.

Back Cover Photograph: *Osprey Alert by* author, copyright 2008.

Photo designs: Jim Primock

Final manuscript preparation: Dianne H. Ewing

Printed in the United States
212033BV00002B/4/P

9 781440 102677